CHALK DUST

Memories & Milestones

Created by

Lauren Roberts

First Edition

PAGE PUBLISHING, INC.
New York, NY

First originally published by Page Publishing, Inc. 2019

ISBN 978-1-64462-626-9 (Hardcover)

Printed in the United States of America

Dedication

This book is dedicated to my amazing parents, Mike and Cherrel, who have been by my side cheering me on through each and every memory and milestone of my life from day one. I would not be the person I am today without the both of you.

First Day of School

Year: ______________________

School: ______________________

Grade: ______________________

Teacher: ______________________

Age: ______________________

Height: ______________________

Future Career: ______________________

Favorite Subject: ______________________

Favorite Book: ______________________

Hobbies: ______________________

First Day of School Picture

Signature:

Last Day of School

Last Day of School Picture

Favorite Memories From This School Year:

Summer Plans:

Notes From The Teacher

Notes From The Proud Parent(s)

First Day of School

Year:

___

School:

___

Grade:

___

Teacher:

___

Age:

___

Height:

___

Future Career:

___

Favorite Subject:

___

Favorite Book:

___

Hobbies:

___

First Day of School Picture

Signature:

Last Day of School Picture

Last Day of School

Favorite Memories From This School Year:

____

____

____

____

____

Summer Plans:

____

____

____

____

Notes From The Teacher

Notes From The Proud Parent(s)

First Day of School

Year: ______________________

School: ______________________

Grade: ______________________

Teacher: ______________________

Age: ______________________

Height: ______________________

Future Career: ______________________

Favorite Subject: ______________________

Favorite Book: ______________________

Hobbies: ______________________

First Day of School Picture

Signature:

Last Day of School Picture

Last Day of School

Favorite Memories From This School Year:

Summer Plans:

Notes From The Teacher

Notes From The Proud Parent(s)

First Day of School

Age:

Height:

Future Career:

Year:

School:

Grade:

Teacher:

Favorite Subject:

Favorite Book:

Hobbies:

First Day of School Picture

Signature:

Last Day of School

Last Day of School Picture

Favorite Memories From This School Year:

Summer Plans:

Notes From The Teacher

Notes From The Proud Parent(s)

First Day of School

Year: ______________________

School: ______________________

Grade: ______________________

Teacher: ______________________

Age: ______________________

Height: ______________________

Future Career: ______________________

First Day of School Picture

Favorite Subject: ______________________

Favorite Book: ______________________

Hobbies: ______________________

Signature:

Last Day of School

Last Day of School Picture

Favorite Memories From This School Year:

Summer Plans:

Notes From The Teacher

Notes From The Proud Parent(s)

First Day of School

Age: ______________________

Height: ______________________

Future Career: ______________________

Year: ______________________

School: ______________________

Grade: ______________________

Teacher: ______________________

Favorite Subject: ______________________

Favorite Book: ______________________

Hobbies: ______________________

First Day of School Picture

Signature:

Last Day of School

Last Day of School Picture

Favorite Memories From This School Year:

Summer Plans:

Notes From The Teacher

Notes From The Proud Parent(s)

First Day of School

Age: ______

Height: ______

Future Career: ______

Year: ______

School: ______

Grade: ______

Teacher: ______

Favorite Subject: ______

Favorite Book: ______

Hobbies: ______

First Day of School Picture

Signature: ______

Last Day of School

Last Day of School Picture

Favorite Memories From This School Year:

Summer Plans:

Notes From The Teacher

Notes From The Proud Parent(s)

First Day of School

Year: ____________________

School: ____________________

Grade: ____________________

Teacher: ____________________

Age: ____________________

Height: ____________________

Future Career: ____________________

Favorite Subject: ____________________

Favorite Book: ____________________

Hobbies: ____________________

First Day of School Picture

Signature:

Last Day of School Picture

Last Day of School

Favorite Memories From This School Year:

Summer Plans:

Notes From The Teacher

Notes From The Proud Parent(s)

First Day of School

Age:

Height:

Future Career:

Year:

School:

Grade:

Teacher:

Favorite Subject:

Favorite Book:

Hobbies:

First Day of School Picture

Signature:

Last Day of School

Last Day of School Picture

Favorite Memories From This School Year:

Summer Plans:

Notes From The Teacher

Notes From The Proud Parent(s)

First Day of School

Year: ______

School: ______

Grade: ______

Teacher: ______

Age: ______

Height: ______

Future Career: ______

Favorite Subject: ______

Favorite Book: ______

Hobbies: ______

First Day of School Picture

Signature: ______

Last Day of School

Last Day of School Picture

Favorite Memories From This School Year:

Summer Plans:

Notes From The Teacher

Notes From The Proud Parent(s)

First Day of School

Year: ______________________

School: ______________________

Grade: ______________________

Teacher: ______________________

Age: ______________________

Height: ______________________

Future Career: ______________________

Favorite Subject: ______________________

Favorite Book: ______________________

Hobbies: ______________________

First Day of School Picture

Signature:

Last Day of School

Last Day of School Picture

Favorite Memories From This School Year:

Summer Plans:

Notes From The Teacher

Notes From The Proud Parent(s)

First Day of School

Year: ______________________

School: ______________________

Grade: ______________________

Teacher: ______________________

Age: ______________________

Height: ______________________

Future Career: ______________________

Favorite Subject: ______________________

Favorite Book: ______________________

Hobbies: ______________________

First Day of School Picture

Signature:

Last Day of School

Last Day of School Picture

Favorite Memories From This School Year:

Summer Plans:

Notes From The Teacher

Notes From The Proud Parent(s)

First Day of School

Age: ____________________

Height: ____________________

Future Career: ____________________

Year: ____________________

School: ____________________

Grade: ____________________

Teacher: ____________________

Favorite Subject: ____________________

Favorite Book: ____________________

Hobbies: ____________________

First Day of School Picture

Signature:

Last Day of School

Last Day of School Picture

Favorite Memories From This School Year:

Summer Plans:

Notes From The Teacher

Notes From The Proud Parent(s)

First Day of School

Year: ______________________

School: ______________________

Grade: ______________________

Teacher: ______________________

Age: ______________________

Height: ______________________

Future Career: ______________________

Favorite Subject: ______________________

Favorite Book: ______________________

Hobbies: ______________________

First Day of School Picture

Signature:

Last Day of School

Last Day of School Picture

Favorite Memories From This School Year:

Summer Plans:

Notes From The Teacher

Notes From The Proud Parent(s)

First Day of School

Year: ____________________

School: ____________________

Grade: ____________________

Teacher: ____________________

Age: ____________________

Height: ____________________

Future Career: ____________________

Favorite Subject: ____________________

Favorite Book: ____________________

Hobbies: ____________________

First Day of School Picture

Signature:

Last Day of School

Last Day of School Picture

Favorite Memories From This School Year:

Summer Plans:

Notes From The Teacher

About The Author

I am a graduate of Saegertown High School and Edinboro University with a degree in Elementary Education. My teaching career was spent in first and second grade at South Conway Elementary in South Carolina, a school with some of the most talented and dedicated teachers and loving students eager to learn. I learned a great deal from both in my years there and consider them all family. I now live a blessed life in Pennsylvania with my favorite people surrounding me each and every day. I am married to the love of my life, Dusty. He is a constant source of joy and humor in my life, he is my most trusted confidant and best friend. I am the mother of our two sweet boys, Blake and Grayson. They are my greatest accomplishments in life and I am amazed by them daily. Sharing my life and love with the three of them is a blessing beyond words.

CPSIA information can be obtained
at www.ICGtesting.com
Printed in the USA
BVHW060607181218
535823BV00002B/2/P

9 781644 626269